Touching the World of Angels

❦

HOW MY DAUGHTER'S SHORT LIFE CHANGED MINE

To two beautiful people,
Remember what is soul,
That is life.

Seth

Touching the World of Angels

HOW MY DAUGHTER'S SHORT LIFE
CHANGED MINE

by
Seth Clyman

First published 2007

ISBN 978-1-60091-038-8

The author can be contacted at:

POB 27477
Jerusalem 91273
Israel

author@sethclyman.com

Distributed by:

Israel Book Shop
501 Prospect Street
Lakewood, NJ 08701

Tel: 732-901-3009   Fax: 732-901-4012

info@israelbookshoppublications.com
www.israelbookshoppublications.com

Printed in Israel

To Ellen

Every day, as we continue to live out our story,
it becomes clearer that I am truly blessed
to share my life with you.

To my children

Here is the story
of what your baby sister left behind.
I wrote it for you.
I'm so proud of you all.

Rabbi Zev Leff

Rabbi, Moshav Matityahu
Rosh HaYeshiva, Yeshiva Gedola Matityahu

Dear Friends,

I have read the manuscript of *Touching the World of Angels* by Seth Clyman and have found it very inspiring.

Having lost a granddaughter of nine months, the subject is close to me. We are enjoined to be *"nosei b'ol im chaviero,"* to literally help carry another's yoke. This goes beyond sympathy and even empathy. We are also enjoined to learn and gain inspiration from the trials and tribulations of others, to enhance our service to and relationship with God.

Mr. Clyman has poignantly shared with us his experiences and feelings over the loss of his baby daughter. Through this account we can be sensitized to the feelings of others who, *lo aleinu,* suffer a similar loss. We can also glean many lessons and much inspiration.

I recommend this book as an effective tool in enhancing one's spirituality.

Sincerely,
With Torah blessings,

Zev Leff

In loving memory of our

Yosef Chaim

His short time with us
will remain with us forever.

The Serruya family
Toronto

In memory of

Joseph Berman

a man who gave of his heart,
from his heart,
helping more people in one lifetime
than most do in many.

Contents

The Dive

I WAS REALLY looking forward to it. I'd read about it, seen pictures, and now I couldn't wait to see it with my own eyes. Ras Mohammed, on the southeast Sinai Peninsula, has some of the best diving in the world, with pristine, clear waters and spectacular marine life.

We finally got there after a long, hot drive. Saudi Arabia, on the other side of the gulf, looked like a Hollywood backdrop. It was so beautiful, so inviting. The water beckoned to us.

We first had to walk out on a shelf that stretched for a few hundred yards, wading through water up to our knees. We were a small group, but I went off on my own. When I approached the end, I was overcome by the

13

eerieness of the deep water — it was so quiet. A manta ray jumped out of the water in front of me and disappeared off the shelf into the depths. My pulse began to race. I had almost stepped on it.

Soon I could tell by the color of the water that I was where I had longed to be. Now it was just over and down.

I looked out over the water. I couldn't help remembering what had happened to my friend Dave.

While diving in this area, Dave had noticed an ominous shadow between him and his boat. The shadow proved to be a very big shark. "Should I go for the boat, go for the shore, or wait it out?" he wondered. The shark seemed interested in an encounter as it circled between him and the boat.

Realizing the shark could stay underwater much longer than he could, Dave decided he didn't want to wait around to see how this would develop. He dropped everything he could, surfaced slowly, and began swimming as soon as he hit the top. He never looked back. It was do or die.

When he made it to the shore, Dave collapsed. His entire body was shaking. He never saw his boat again.

Here I was, now, in the same spot. No boat, just me. I plunged into the crystal blue, and soon all I saw was bubbles.

It was so beautiful, just looking at the side of the underwater cliff that went down into the depths as far as one could see. A world of splendor. So quiet. The coral, *the colors, the fish. It was better than the books. It was well worth the drive and the dive.*

Every few minutes I checked below and behind me. I was aware that my back was facing a world that was not mine. I knew they were out there. The book said so, and so did Dave. I was taught never to give your back to someone you don't trust.

As I enjoyed the breathtaking underwater scenery, I couldn't help but think about how vulnerable we are when we venture into unfamiliar territory. Swimming in unknown waters, we're not at home or in charge. In such a world we must be careful. There are consequences.

Suddenly, something entered my space. I couldn't see it, but it was fast approaching. I turned around and looked out into the blue expanse. Nothing. Whatever it was, it felt too close.

Panic set in. I realized that I had forgotten to check below, but before I could look into the depths to see what was closing in on me, I felt a grip on my calf. It began to shake me.

Everything went black. Where was I?

"Get up, get up! People are waiting in the living room," said my brother Joel, letting go of my leg. "For a twenty-minute nap, you looked like you were in a pretty deep sleep. I'll tell them you'll be out in a minute."

Oh yes, how vulnerable we are, I thought, as the dream faded away...and the last few days, the days that shattered my world, all came back to me crystal clear.

Preface

LOSING A BABY is like getting hit with a knockout punch and not knowing where it came from. When you come to, everything is hazy. Out of the fog, you slowly come back to yourself.

In the years following my baby's passing, life and death took on different shades. My life — and my baby's, as short as it was — took on new meaning.

When someone goes to sleep, you expect him to wake up, especially if that someone is a baby. Babies wake up with big smiles, or crying to be fed, or just wanting to be taken out of the crib. But they wake up. When your baby doesn't, your life changes. It has to.

I suddenly found myself, against my will, amongst

the ranks of the devastated. I want to share with you the challenges that I faced as I was initiated into this select club. I was floored, and that is exactly where I found myself sitting during the seven days of shiva.

I felt those seven days paralleled the seven days of Creation, where the first day, the "beginning," was "void and desolate," but by the seventh, a whole world had been created out of nothing. Each day of Creation ends with the words, "It was evening and it was morning." In biblical terms, the day starts at nightfall, with darkness and confusion, and moves toward light, toward understanding and clarity. I felt this image was a metaphor for my grief, and I have made use of it in this book.

When crib death showed up on our doorstep, it brought void and desolation. Yet it catalyzed a dimensional shift in my life.

I want to share with you this week, which launched a journey I couldn't have begun on my own.

The End

NO ONE ELSE was at the cemetery as the sun started to set. Just the driver and a man holding a small bundle. They approached the hole, dug within the last hour. The freshly turned ground was mixed with rocks. The bundle was placed carefully in the hole and immediately covered with earth and left unmarked.

If only we could understand the impact this bundle would have on us and those around us. If only we could fathom its power. The power of creation. The power of eternity.

At the same time, not so far away, someone is crying, and the power is overwhelming — if only we could harness it.

The tears keep coming. It's hitting hard. Channel the impact, and come out alive.

The Beginning

1:43 p.m. PARAMEDICS RECEIVE CALL ABOUT BABY IN DISTRESS.

1:44 p.m. AMBULANCE LEAVES STATION WITH FULL TEAM.

1:54 p.m. AMBULANCE ARRIVES ON SCENE.

"We've been looking for you," the office manager said. "You have a call. You can pick it up privately in my office."

"Hello?" I said into the receiver.

I recognized my neighbor's voice at the other end. "You should come home right away," she said with forced calmness. "Your baby isn't well....Please don't ask any questions, just come home as soon as you can."

21

"Okay. But what — "

"Don't ask," she cut me off. "Just come home." She hung up.

I called home. No answer. Not a good sign.

I tried the upstairs neighbor to get more information. A child picked up the phone and told me her mother was down the street. An ambulance siren in the background was all I needed to hear. Numb but composed, I turned and walked through the office. Everyone knew something was very wrong.

2:09 p.m. AMBULANCE RUSHES BABY TO HOSPITAL, SIREN BLARING.

I jumped into a cab. The twenty-minute ride home seemed like forever. I sat there next to the driver, deep in thought. My wife, the kids, the baby.... But I remember two things distinctly.

The first was a miniature black and yellow soccer ball dangling from the rearview mirror. Week after week this sphere has millions of people around the world jumping and screaming when it makes its way into a twenty-four-by-eight-foot net. I thought it was funny that this ball, the cause of all the excitement, was dangling at the end of a string. Just hanging there... right in front of my eyes.

The second thing I recall, approaching my neighborhood, was the wailing of the siren as an ambulance whizzed past us in the opposite direction. I knew Ellen and the baby were in there, but in the time it would take us to turn around, we would lose sight of them. The ambulance was going so fast…and to which hospital? I felt so helpless. Now I wasn't sure who was dangling from a string — the baby, the ball, or me. I let the driver in on what was happening. We were just a few minutes from home.

2:16 p.m. AMBULANCE ARRIVES AT HOSPITAL.

As we pulled into my street, it seemed too quiet for the middle of the day, especially for a cul-de-sac where over four hundred children live.

Two women were waiting outside my house. "Just turn around and go to Hadassah Hospital," they said.

The Last
Good-bye

THE EMERGENCY ROOM was also too quiet. For a place usually bustling with doctors, nurses, and patients, it was as if someone had pulled the plug — on the room and my baby daughter.

I spotted my wife. Looking at her, I could only imagine what she had gone through till she got here. The baby...I could tell she was surrounded by a team of doctors, but I could barely see her. They noticed me. The father had come. But no one had time to speak to me, as they were so busy with her.

She was so little on that table, hidden by everyone's

hands. I prayed for a miracle, though deep down I knew it was too late. They kept trying to get a pulse, something, anything. It was all so fast, from that phone call to the emergency room. All I wanted to hear was a beep from that ticker-tape machine everyone was checking constantly. I could see them trying any and every possible way to save her. They refused to give up. No one wanted to give up on a baby. But, finally, the head doctor spoke:

"*Enough*. There's nothing left to do."

Slowly and quietly, the medical team peeled off, until she was left alone.

They couldn't get her to breathe.

You could have sliced the air in the room.

Everyone on the floor spoke in hushed voices. My little girl lying there dwarfed everyone's problems. We had been married seven years and had a beautiful family. Life had been very good to us. In six days it would be our anniversary. We'd felt truly blessed and were very appreciative of it, knowing that not everyone gets even part of their wish list answered. Everyone has challenges in life, and we'd certainly had our share, but something here had seriously backfired. Something had gone very, very wrong.

Babies don't die; they're supposed to grow. It shouldn't happen like this. Children should bury their parents.

What now? Our children were our first priority — the ones at home and the baby here in the hospital — so we had no choice but to deal with our feelings later. We decided Ellen should go home to the kids, and I should stay.

I had never arranged a funeral, let alone for my own daughter. So I called Yale Burns, a very close and knowledgeable friend who knew the baby had been in danger. He picked up the phone and the words came out of my mouth:

"My baby died."

I sensed his pain and courage as he answered, "I guess God didn't want her to live anymore."

This thought would dive-bomb in and out of my conciousness throughout the next few weeks. After I called the burial society and made arrangements for the pickup, all I could see were my tears. Endless waves of salt water.

I WASN'T THE FIRST

John waited restlessly with his brother and two close friends. He had barely slept since his son's birth the previous day. Between traveling to see his wife and the baby and trying to keep up with some very pressing matters, the physical and emotional walls were closing in.

Shifting nervously in his chair, he peered every

now and then through the window of the intensive-care unit where a team of doctors and nurses huddled around his baby, just twenty-five hours old. The infant's fate seemed to be out of their hands, beyond men and machines. Deep, deep in his heart he was praying. Despite all his connections, he had nowhere else to turn. His wife wasn't even aware of how bad the situation was.

At 4:04 in the morning, the doctor came out and told the father, "I'm sorry. We did all we could. The baby's struggle to keep breathing was just too much for his heart."

John might have been the most powerful person in the world, but here he was helpless. He had lost this battle.

Stunned, he walked away from the doctor. He needed to be alone. He disappeared behind the door leading into the hospital boiler room. He stayed inside …alone.

Tears flowed from the eyes of a father who would never get to know his son, never get to share those special moments together — playing ball, going fishing, walking through the forest, teaching him how to swim …being there when a father needs to be, teaching him about life, or just watching him grow up. The tears kept coming.

Finally, John emerged from his seclusion. His younger brother Bobby put his arm around him and they walked out of the hospital. He now had to go tell his wife, Jackie, who was at another hospital recuperating from the birth.

Three and a half months later, a message would come crackling over the Secret Service wire: "Lancer is dead." Two bullets from a lone assassin had killed this father, John F. Kennedy, the 34th president of the United States.

Within half an hour, someone from the burial society came to the emergency room. Together we walked out the back entrance of the hospital. My daughter was now a little bundle on a trolley. When we reached his van, the driver went back inside to finish signing the release papers. For the first time since hearing the word *"Enough,"* I found myself outside. Fresh air, deep breaths, and sun. I felt on more personal terms with these surroundings.

As I stood there waiting, I realized I had to do it. I hadn't held my daughter since the night before, and I knew this would be my last chance, my last time. My little bundle of joy. I picked her up and held her close. Me, her, and the sky. In a few hours I would give her back, but I wouldn't be giving her up. She would be elsewhere, but I would still have her. She was passing from our world to the world soon to be hers. I couldn't explain it, but I felt it.

It seemed that only yesterday I had left this hospital through the front door, holding her as a newborn. We were bringing our new daughter home. Now I was leaving the same hospital, holding her, but this time through the back door. And this time we weren't going home.

Through my tears, what kept coming to mind was the famous image of the soldier falling at Gallipoli, arms open wide and screaming as he took his last look at this world. The word "why" was all I could hear. Holding my baby daughter, no screaming was necessary. I couldn't have gotten the word out even if I'd tried.

The sky looked down upon me, standing outside the hospital, and heard every thought that was racing through my mind. I felt I was rapidly entering a dimension of reality that had always been there, but I had never taken the time to notice. I had never felt so helpless and small.

WORLD OF ANGELS I

When it was time for God to give out jobs to the angels, they all crowded around. One by one, job descriptions were read out, and positions were assigned to angels of joy, of growth, of wealth, of laughter...until it came time to appoint the angel of death.

"Why me?" asked the "lucky one," backing away. "What type of job is that for an angel?! To bring tears, sadness, and mourning...?"

"Don't worry," God replied. "They'll blame themselves or someone else. No one will ever blame you."

We drove through the streets of Jerusalem. I had never really thought about what it must be like to ride in those big burial society vans. Now I didn't get much time to take in the experience. The driver turned around and said, "The funeral will be at 4:30."

Why was he telling me? Where did he think I was going? I thought I was staying with him. Me, him, and my daughter.

"You have to go to the Ministry of Health and get the burial license," he explained.

"Me?!"

"Make sure you get back by 4:30."

Bureaucracy...this was too much. For the next few minutes I just stared at my baby daughter, wrapped in white. Then the driver dropped me off right in the middle of downtown Jerusalem, with traffic galore. I was a block away from the open-air market, with all its honking and bustling. It was one of the last places I wanted to be.

I had lost a world, and it was driving away in that dark-blue van. Now I had to get a piece of paper allowing me to bury my daughter, as there was no suspicion of foul play. If there had been no foul play, why was I so full of questions?

I felt numb and so alone. If the death of a little baby girl isn't foul play, then what is?

I imagined bumping into a friend. "What's new?" he would ask me.

"Not much," I would respond. "I'm just on the way

31

to my daughter's funeral. Want to come? Let's get a cab. Don't worry, they won't start without me."

I don't know how I did it. But soon enough, burial permit in hand, I was in a taxi headed to my daughter's funeral. Yes, I would be on time.

A crowd waited at the funeral home. As we pulled up, I began recognizing friends and family. Getting out of the car, I wasn't sure what to expect. A few people gravitated toward me. My friend Simon asked me very softly what had happened. That's the very question I had been wanting to scream! But it was the wrong confrontation for me now. Tears came pouring out, and I quickly walked away, surrounded by more friends.

The next thing I knew, my wife and I were led into a room where the baby was. There we were to ask her forgiveness for any wrong we might have done her during her short stay with us. So small, so quiet, so powerful. The moment is etched in my mind forever. I knew this would be my last time seeing her in this world, and I had better make it count. But I couldn't; the dam burst. Tears again.

I somehow managed to ask forgiveness from a two-month-old. How could she even understand me? But I was about to find out that souls are mature from the second they enter our bodies; only appearances are deceiving.

There were no eulogies. Within a few minutes, a man from the burial society gently placed our baby back in the van and prepared to leave for the cemetery. As the van slowly pulled away, Mr. Francis, an old family friend, put his arm around my shoulders and urged us, as parents of the baby, not to go to the cemetery now or ever. We could go now if we wanted, or find out where she was buried and go in the future, but the custom was otherwise. It was better, he said, to just go home and start sitting shiva.

The parents shouldn't go to the burial?! His words hit like a ton of bricks. No grave to visit? No place to cherish? Our daughter would simply disappear in that big, blue van forever? I had arranged for my daughter's funeral, but I had almost no part in it. Standing there in pain and confusion, I watched the van drive off. I felt like an anvil being struck by a hammer.

I know now that if the hammer hadn't hit then, when I was seeing my daughter for the last time, it would have been even harder to heal. Reality was beginning to set in. She was leaving and I was staying. All so fast, a blur. What had just happened to her and us would soon be clear, if a few years counted as "soon." My friend Ezra drove us home. It was a very quiet ride.

As we pulled up to our house, about to submerge ourselves indoors for seven days, I again sensed that eery silence on the street. The angel of death had come much too close for comfort.

We spend most of our lives viewing and understanding the world, with all its props and players, from our comfortable perspective. When we lose a parent, sibling, child, or spouse, that perspective is radically altered, and we are profoundly affected.

According to Jewish law, the mourner sits shiva. For seven days you stay home. You sit on the floor, or on a low chair or surface, as your family, friends, and community come to comfort you. For that week, the stage disappears. You process everything from a new angle, and you see things in a new light.

The week that followed was the longest of my life. I felt as if I was strapped to a rocket and sent into orbit, destined to reenter the Earth's atmosphere only in another seven days. In the meantime I was aboard this projectile; it was hurtling forward, and there was no getting off. Sitting shiva left me no choice but to confront the journey. I couldn't avoid it. I wouldn't. Seated on the floor, I felt weakened, humbled, and exposed. I was facing something larger than life as I'd known it.

FOOD FOR THOUGHT

Dinner was fine Yemenite cuisine. The company was special and the conversation even more so. We found parking right around the corner to boot. When it came to ordering dessert, the waiter suggested the house specialty. We asked what it was. He said that it was for us to figure out. If we could identify this delicacy, dinner would be on the house — an offer we couldn't refuse.

A magnificent dessert was served. Now I knew why the lights were dim. We looked, tasted, smelled, and dissected, but the three of us hadn't a clue. We could have gotten a free meal, but we couldn't guess dessert.

When the waiter returned to hear what we thought we'd just eaten, we were speechless. With a smooth movement of the hand, a little tray with three mints and the bill was placed on the table. "My friends," he revealed with a smile, "you just had a radish. Please come again."

It's amazing how skillfully a true identity can be hidden.

During dinner the couple I was dining with asked me what it means when parents lose a child. I gave the matter a passing thought. Little did I realize I would be asking myself the same question fifteen years later.

Day One

THE SHIVA BEGINS

ONE OF THE first people to come to our house that evening after the funeral was Mr. Raphael, a neighbor. He sat to my right as I looked up at him.

Mr. Raphael is a very well-respected, sought-after community leader. I was awed by his presence, by his coming to be with me. We have since developed a relationship, but up to that point I don't think we had really spoken to each other.

After asking him a few questions about the customs and conventions of shiva, we sort of looked at one another. Just he and I. My eyes were pleading, "Help me, I just lost my baby daughter!" He bit his lip, closed his eyes, and wept for a few seconds. A great man sat there crying with me. The two of us. I can still see it now.

I felt that life was offering me the challenge, saying, "There is a big ladder before you. Welcome to the next rung."

"We'll talk," Mr. Raphael said as he stood up to leave. "It's too early."

Was he ever right.

Ellen and I still had not really been able to speak with each other. Between all the friends visiting and phoning and bringing over food, there was a lot going on. We would just have to wait till the day ended and everyone went home. We didn't realize this day would last much longer than twenty-four hours.

The children were farmed out to friends for the week, except for Avi, who had chicken pox. His presence was the only sign of normalcy in the house. The two older ones, Tehilla and Emuna, understood that something had changed at home, and I was sure we would be seeing them tomorrow.

When sitting shiva, the mourner doesn't greet visitors. There's no small talk. I initiated any conversation. If I didn't talk, it was because I couldn't, but it meant a lot that someone was there. I needed contact with the outside world, but on my terms. The hardest conversations were the ones where nothing was said. There was nothing to be said. People came because they wanted me to know they were there, and that's what I needed. With some people I cried — it was good; it was necessary. We all cry, either outwardly or inwardly. Sometimes both are best.

I recalled an article about two close friends meeting for what they knew would be the last time, as one was very sick. They just sat together in silence. Sometimes there's no closer relationship than one in which nothing need be said. When professional athletes have practiced a play hundreds of times, when ice skaters have rehearsed a routine for hours on end, the harmony and execution are flawless. They are perfectly in sync. Sitting shiva creates a synchronization of souls.

The deceased effectively binds together those he or she leaves behind. Without ever having "practiced," we survivors know why we're together, and there is no need to speak. The silence can be earth-shattering.

When we spoke during the week, it was about the baby, about life. People bring it out of you because you are sitting opposite the loss.

All the mirrors in a Jewish house of mourning are covered. To really look at yourself, Judaism tells the mourner, you don't need mirrors. Don't worry about what people think of you; examine how you feel about yourself. Who is the person you really want others to see? Have you ever really thought about who you are and who you appear to be? Who is the real you? A mourner is at a disadvantage, sitting low and devastated, and there is no room for pretense. People want to be with the real you, and sometimes that is the hardest person to be.

All the world's a stage, but not this week and hopefully not for the rest of your life. When you lose your most precious possession, it brings out the real you. Can you face it? Can you deal with it? Where do you start? Where do you find the strength to bear what is almost unbearable?

I woke up in the middle of the first night. What a dream! And when I awoke, I was sure I had walked into another dream. In the living room, a dim light emanated from the memorial candle that was to remain lit the entire week. It gave off just enough light in the darkness of the moment. I looked outside at the mountains in the distance. There was a full moon. Everything was crisp, clear, quiet, and so peaceful. There was a certain awesomeness to the whole scene. Back inside all was still. The flickering candle, the shadows.... I sat down on the floor where I would be sitting for the next few days and thought...and thought and thought. I was deep in the forest.

WORLD OF ANGELS II

In my dream, I sat in the second row of spectators in the ultimate courtroom. They were all there, finally on trial:

the most evil and ruthless murderers throughout history, responsible for so much pain, agony, and death. Now, in living color for everyone to see, all they could muster were blank stares. These evil, two-legged animals couldn't hurt anyone now. History was written around these beasts. Darkness belonged to them.

All the "truths" they had propounded while alive were now exposed as big lies. There was nothing for them to say as they all prepared to meet their Creator, to whom, to their surprise, they were accountable for their actions. I felt I was about to see justice done.

But as I watched, someone was missing. If they could track down all these monsters, why not the one who took my daughter? Suddenly, a barrage of questions shook me like an avalanche of bitter injustice. She didn't just die by herself. Where was my daughter's killer?

My thoughts led me down a corridor, where I found myself involved in a confrontation I mistakenly thought I was prepared for.

"You wanted to speak to Me?" an overpowering voice thundered.

Me and my grandiose thoughts! Now I was quite sure I wasn't ready for this meeting. I would have liked a little more time to prepare.

I recognized the voice, having heard it on and off throughout my life. So why was I shaking?

"After all the years we've spent together, you finally come to Me? I've been so good to you, but you've been *too busy to notice. Oh, you certainly appreciated everything and recognized how lucky you were, but did you ever really believe Someone was taking care of you? People sometimes refer to Me as their 'Father in Heaven,' but, really, they treat Me more like their 'Grandfather in Heaven.' They expect Me to be all fun and games.*

"But do yourself a favor and remember, I'm your Father in Heaven. I'm with you for better and for what you call worse. I'm always here for you; you just have to call. When you are up to your neck in mud, I'll get even dirtier than you to get you out. But as I clean you off, I might let you have it for getting dirty in the first place. And don't expect lollipops from Me all the time. That wouldn't be good for you. I'll always give you just what you need, when you need it, because no one loves you more than I.

"Now, what did you want to see Me about?"

Was I big enough to spar with God? Did I really want all the answers? Would I then be content? When was the last time I truly thanked my Creator, Sustainer, and Supervisor for all the good in my life? And if I did thank Him, did I ever think maybe I wasn't worthy of it? That maybe, just once, I had received someone else's order instead? Now, in my grief, when I'm sure I've been wronged, I demand vengeance. But have I ever expressed my thanks to Him with the same depth of emotion?

Maybe I'm nearsighted and see only part of the picture.

If I had all the answers handed to me on a silver platter, maybe I would pass the test of life with flying colors, but I wouldn't learn anything. Only by working it out for yourself will you achieve true understanding. We want our children to figure out their homework on their own. It would be so much easier just to tell them the answers. But then, would they really be passing the test?

How hard am I willing to work? How badly do I want to meet the challenge of life?

I had a strange feeling I wasn't alone in the room. That little flame gave off so much light. It seemed to be trying to chase away the darkness. I became very aware of my heartbeat, realizing it had never stopped. It just kept going, seemingly on its own. How had that happened?

I wasn't the only one with questions. My neighbor's young daughter, Shiri, asked her mother whether, after the baby was in the ground, dirt covering her eyes and face, she would grow like a flower. Somehow Shiri sensed it wasn't over. It couldn't be over.

It was evening and it was morning,
the first day.

Day Two

THE MORNING AFTER that strange first night, I woke up early, but Ellen kept sleeping. She was exhausted from the last few months of running around caring for her sick mother. Trips to the hospital, consultations, tests and treatments had occupied the bulk of her time.

We took the baby to see Ellen's mother whenever we could. It always made her feel better. Very few things can give an extremely ill person a lift, but holding her newest grandchild could. Now we had to tell her the bad news.

Ellen was carrying a lot on her shoulders, not to mention Avi's chicken pox. It didn't seem fair that in the midst of doing so much good, showing such care and concern, and giving so much of herself, she should be hit with this. It just didn't seem right.

I found myself alone in the living room when the first visitor came. It was Penny, a family friend I don't see or speak with too often, but with whom there's still a special friendship. The early-morning sun was shining through the window, and the room was full of light. It was a beautiful day. Taking a deep breath, I made my first effort to talk about what happened, about yesterday. I was still there. After managing just a few words, I broke down.

During the first three days of shiva, it's customary that only close friends and family come to comfort the mourner. With them you can attempt to reenter this world, to return to society. You can talk to them; you can cry with them.

I was starting to touch something beyond. For these seven long days, the more I spoke, the more I struggled. In the face of death, I grappled with the meaning of life. When all the "ceremony" is over, reality remains. My baby daughter had to die for me to finally, sincerely ask myself these questions. The challenge was laid out in front of me, and I wasn't going anywhere that week. I had the time.

An old friend came and told me how, when he sat shiva, he couldn't deal with his loss, so he didn't. He never spoke about his departed, and he avoided the sensitive issues.

I felt like telling him, "Why don't you just pull up a

pillow and sit down on the floor next to me?" He needed to start making peace with his loss. I could feel his pain still eating away at him, because I could feel mine.

HIGH-WIRE ACT

Four years of hard work on a multimillion-dollar building project, designed by a world-renowned architect and located in one of the most beautiful, historic, and emotionally charged sites in the world — the Old City of Jerusalem. I was one of the project coordinators.

We had a deadline. The main benefactors were coming with a mission of almost a hundred people to see "their building." A few sleepless nights and we had it pretty much together.

The morning of their visit, I arrived early to make sure everything was ready. We were going to pull it off. An hour before they were to arrive, the workers were applying the finishing touches. It was a beautiful day.

I had never met Mr. and Mrs. Dan, the principal visionaries who had seen this project through. I had heard a lot about them, though, and was looking forward to showing them around.

As I looked down onto the road leading to the site, I noticed no traffic. That was very unusual for one of the most visited places in the world. What was going on? Then someone told me that a head of state, whom I knew was in town, might be coming to the Old City later in the day, so all the roads were blocked off for security reasons. I guessed our group would just have to walk in — which they did.

Then came the phone call that really made my day.

The Dans were at the top of the long flight of steps leading down to the building. Did I have any idea how to get Mrs. Dan to the site, since she was in a wheelchair?

What was I supposed to do? I wondered in exasperation. Take out my flying carpet?

I looked up to the heavens and said, "God, You have to help me with this one!"

Seconds later, I saw the answer. There was Hank, ten stories up in the air, manning his crane. He would stay up there all day. He had lifted tons of cement and steel at this site over the years, but now he was about to carry a different type of load. It was a moment of insanity, I must admit. He could have lost his license, and I could have lost more than that, but I was going to get Mrs. Dan to her building.

I arranged to have the crane set its carriage on the terrace of the building's lower reception area. This was showtime. I hopped in and gave Hank the thumbs-up. He had a big smile on his face. We radioed him to transport me to the street above the building, pick up a visitor, and bring us back down to the front terrace. He loved it.

Up I went, sitting in this open box — its sides only twenty inches high — suspended in midair by four steel cables.

I never would have thought it would be so peaceful

up there. *Too terrified to look down, I just looked out as this massive steel arm swung me over to my destination. I could see for hundreds of miles. It was incredible. But I was scared stiff. Who had talked me into this?*

The Dans couldn't believe it as I landed right in front of them. I felt like one of those aliens walking off the spaceship to meet the earthlings. "Nice to meet you," I greeted Mrs. Dan. "I've come to take you to your building."

We maneuvered her in and secured the wheelchair. The rest of the party watched us lift off. What a way to start a dedication ceremony!

Up and over, just the two of us. I was glad it was happening so fast. My stomach was turning, We engaged in a little small talk, but what struck me was that she wasn't afraid at all. She looked pretty much like a queen sitting there, flying through the air. As I looked up at her, framed by the royal blue sky, she looked quite regal. Seated on her "throne," she seemed so serene. Not one bit afraid. I'll never forget that.

I realized that when you're being helped all the time, as she was, you begin trusting people.

We think we control the world around us. We may have to be hoisted ten stories in midair, dangling from steel lifelines, to realize that at least sometimes we have to rely on someone else.

How about breathing? On whom do we rely for that?

As we swung over the building, the people down below on the terrace went wild. Word had spread that this was going to be a grand entrance. Hank gave us a beautiful landing. It was a ride and a lesson I'll never forget.

I wondered Who was taking me for this big ride and what He wanted from me now that He certainly had my attention.

I was visited by a very special friend, Mr. Orlander. He is one of the people I seek out when I need advice about life. I deeply respect the wisdom of these people, and if I disagree with their insights, I question myself before questioning them. In time, they have proven right.

"People want to know exactly what happened," I told him. "It usually comes up somehow, and it hurts. Why do they want to know? It seems so unimportant, at least this week."

He looked at me understandingly. "I don't want to know what happened," he replied quietly. "I didn't come here to hear that. The mechanics don't really matter."

How right he was. Though it would take years, it seemed so much more important to try and grasp what it all *meant*. A soul that had to be here briefly came down in the form of a beautiful baby and then returned to the world it came from. How a death takes place is not the point. How a person lived and what he or she accomplished is what really matters. But what did my daughter accomplish?

All souls come down to this world with a mission. Some missions take a long lifetime to complete, some take a few years, and some take not much time at all. Whatever our mission, once it's completed, there's no longer any need to be here.

"How do we talk to our children?" I continued. "How do we tell them what happened to their baby sister?"

"Just tell them the truth: 'Your baby sister has left this world and has gone back to the Creator of all souls. She no longer has to be here with us, and you now have a sister in Heaven.'"

He paused, and my eyes opened wider.

"You seem surprised. Don't worry, the little ones can handle the loss. We're the ones with the problem. They see life through pure eyes. When it's time to cry, they cry; when it's time to smile, they smile; when it's time to laugh, they laugh. We're the ones who put on the facades, and, over the years, we become very good at it."

"So how do *we* start dealing with loss?" I asked.

"We can begin by just taking better notice of a baby," Mr. Orlander said. "Babies can lie on their backs, and once they find their hand, they can play with it for hours. They find it simply fascinating. They can play with a rattle forever. What a world...when they can focus...when they can recognize voices. They don't need much.

"We adults need better toys than our hands, eyes,

and ears. It bores us to look at something so 'simple' as a hand. So what if it makes every movement we desire? We wouldn't expect anything less. It grasps, it points, it touches, it feels, it senses. Could you imagine waking up and trying to grab a cup of coffee and finding that your hand doesn't move? You try again...nothing! What went wrong? 'It's worked my whole life, it's never failed me.' Do you follow?"

"I guess we really take it all for granted," I agreed.

"Absolutely. We end up seeing life the way we would like it to be — and when it isn't, we just make believe it is. How we fool ourselves!"

Sometimes we have to wait until we're at the edge of a cliff, or maybe even on the way down, before we wake up.

"Hi, Daddy!"

There she was, right on cue. School was out, and our oldest daughter, Tehilla, all of seven years old, came in. The baby had actually been born on her birthday. We would always tell Tehilla that the baby was her birthday present.

Ellen told Tehilla and Emuna, our six-year-old, that the baby had gone to a special place in Heaven and was very happy there. They both seemed a bit puzzled, but the idea was planted. We would have to see what would become of it.

Tehilla sat down beside us. There was no one else

in the room.

"Mommy," she asked, "if the baby is happy, how come you and Daddy look so sad?"

"Because we miss her," Ellen explained. "It will take time to get used to her not being here with us. Are you used to it?"

"No. But if she is happy, then I guess we should be happy," our seven-year-old answered. She thought a moment. "Mommy, can I ask you a question?"

"Sure, anything you want."

"Every Friday night, you light two candles for Shabbos, right?"

I saw the question coming. How perceptive these kids can be. This was going to hurt.

"You also light a candle for every one of us kids, right?"

"Right."

"Well, when you lit candles last Shabbos, there was one for the baby, and I remember you had a big smile when you lit it. Mommy, are you going to light a candle for her again this week?"

I looked at Ellen as she hugged Tehilla tight.

"Of course, I'll light a candle for her. I always will. She will always light up our house. Just like all you kids."

Now Tehilla had a big smile. "I can't wait for next Shabbos."

"Why?"

"Because when you light a candle for her and you

smile, you won't be so sad."

I had to look away. It was too much. Children are so real.

"And Daddy?"

"Yes, Tehilla?" I guess it was my turn.

"In case you were wondering, you don't have to buy me another birthday present. She's the best thing you could have given me....Do we have any Popsicles left?"

"Yes, go look in the freezer," Ellen told her, "and don't forget to close the door."

And off she went, leaving us, manhandled by a seven-year-old.

A CHILDREN'S STORY

Ben lived at the edge of town in a big, two-story house. Outside his second-floor bedroom window lay a huge field full of yellow and red flowers in the summer and clean, white snow in the winter.

Ben had a small, gray bird that he kept in a cage. It wasn't handsome, but it could sing a hundred songs. Ben liked the bird's singing. He liked to give it birdseed and water, in two little dishes, and white chalk with which to scratch its claws and beak.

But Ben also liked poking the bird with a stick. Then the bird would squawk and flap its wings and fly around the cage, trying to get away from Ben's stick. But it never could, because the cage was so small, and the stick was long. Sometimes Ben's parents caught him poking the bird and told him to stop, so he did — but only for a few days. Then he would start all over again.

One day, when Ben was giving the bird its water, his brother David called him from downstairs: "Ben, we're going outside to play."

"I'm coming," Ben shouted back. He quickly shut the door of the bird cage and ran downstairs to play with David and their friends in the field.

But Ben hadn't closed the cage door all the way. After a few minutes, the bird noticed the latch wasn't in place. It pushed its beak against the door, and the door swung open. After a few seconds, the bird hopped out. It had never been out of the cage before, and it wasn't used to the feeling. It flapped its wings and flew over to the window. In the field below, it saw the boys playing.

"The window is open, and I can fly out to freedom!" the bird thought.

With a last look at the room and the cage where it had spent its entire life, the bird flapped its wings and flew out over the field where the boys were playing. At that moment, Ben's eyes were following a ball he'd thrown up toward the sky. He noticed a bird flying by, higher than his ball, distancing itself from him and his house. He didn't realize that the bird was his. Only later, when he returned to his room and saw the open window and the open, empty cage, did he discover that his bird had flown away.

At first he was sad. After a few weeks, though, he forgot about it. Several months later, he threw the cage *out and never gave the bird another thought.*

Ben grew up. He did well in school and made his parents proud. At age twenty-three he married. He and his wife brought seven children into the world. He worked hard, provided for his family, and served his community, always volunteering, always there to help friends and strangers alike. After he retired, he continued assisting those in need. He became a grandfather and great-grandfather many times over. He was happy with his life.

One day, when Ben was ninety-one, he felt too weak to get out of bed. His son-in-law called a doctor, who sent Ben to the hospital, but they couldn't help him. With his children at his side, Ben passed away.

Ben's soul left his body and rose from the earth. Soon it arrived in a courtroom where three celestial judges would decide its fate.

"Witnesses for the defense," a clerk announced.

One by one, all the angels created by Ben's good deeds came before the judges. The angels said so many nice things that Ben grew embarrassed. He remembered every act mentioned.

Then the clerk summoned, "Witnesses for the prosecution."

Ben trembled as more angels stepped up. One by one, they presented their devastating testimony, until he wept in shame.

When the final witness had spoken, the judges conferred. Finally, the chief justice announced, "Having ex-

amined the witnesses' testimony, we rule that you may go to Heaven."

"Thank you! Oh, thank you!" Ben cried, lifting his eyes. But something flew between him and the judges and landed between them. It was a bird.

"Who are you?" demanded the chief justice. "What are you doing in this court of law?"

"I am a witness no one called," the bird declared. "But I wish to testify, too — against this man."

"I don't know who this bird is!" protested Ben.

"You don't know me?" squawked the bird. "You don't remember how you poked me with a stick until my feathers fell out and my heart beat so hard I thought I would faint? Don't you remember all the pain you caused me? You treated everyone else so nicely. Everyone else is so happy with you."

"Oh, yes, I remember. But I was just a little boy," Ben demurred.

"You weren't too little to hurt me," the bird retorted.

Ben turned to the judges. "I was only a child. I didn't know I was inflicting so much pain."

The judges huddled. Then the chief justice leaned forward to Ben. "True, you were young. But tormenting animals is a very serious offense."

Ben felt weak and broke out in a sweat.

"Your actions created a flaw in your soul that you must correct. Before entering Heaven you must return to earth — as a bird — and repair the damage."

"Wait a minute, Your Honor!" cried Ben, but suddenly the courtroom disappeared.

A moment later, Ben found himself floating in a round room. It was warm and comfortable. Although suspended in a thick liquid, he had no trouble breathing.

On the contrary, it was quite pleasant.

From day to day, Ben felt himself growing bigger and stronger. Finally, one day he banged his head against the wall of his room. Again and again he banged against the wall until it cracked open. A strong, white light streamed in together with a rush of cool air.

"Where am I?" Ben wanted to say, but only a peep was heard. "I was in an egg," he realized, "and now I've hatched. I'm a baby bird!" Ben opened his mouth and cried out. His mother — a beautiful nightingale — pushed food into his mouth, and he swallowed greedily. He felt better, and he slept.

As time passed, Ben learned to hop and then fly. He quickly became independent and left the nest. As he flew about, he often thought about how he could fix himself so he could make his way back to Heaven. He loved to ponder as he soared high above the trees, floating on the air currents, but he couldn't think of a thing to do. What could a bird do?

When Ben would chirp in desperation, people listened. They would say to one another, "How beautifully that bird sings."

"Who cares about beautiful songs?" Ben would lament. "Listen, I'm Ben! Can't you help me?"

But no one understood him.

Ben grew bitter and disappointed. Eventually he made his home in a poplar tree next to an old house. In the house lived a young man with his nine-year-old son, Adam. The man's wife had died a few years earlier, so he was raising the boy by himself. It was just the two of them in that big, old house.

Ben paid little attention to them. Day by day he felt sorrier and sorrier for himself, and he nested in the tree without making a sound.

Once in a while, he saw a doctor with a thick, black bag entering the house. Through the upstairs window, he watched the doctor examine the boy. He noticed Adam getting paler and thinner. He never came outside to play. Soon Adam began spending most of his time in bed.

One day, Adam and his father left the house in a taxi. Ben heard the father direct the driver to the hospital. In the evening, Adam's father returned home alone. Ben heard him crying in the house.

A few weeks later, Adam returned. Now he lay in bed all day, and his father stayed home to take care of him. Things continued like this for weeks, then months.

One bright, sunny spring morning, after a pleasant night's sleep, Ben thought to himself, "Why be depressed? At least let me be who I am and do what I was created to do. I'm a bird. People say I sing so beautifully, so let me sing to the world."

So he began singing. At first his voice came out somewhat harsh, because he hadn't sung for months.

But soon his songs were like prayers, and he sang them with all his heart.

Adam lay in bed, bored, tired, and hopeless. The doctors thought he wouldn't live more than a few months, so they had sent him home to be more comfortable as he approached his last days.

One day, Adam heard a bird singing outside his window. The sound bothered him, and he wished the bird would go away. But the bird kept singing. Gradually, Adam found himself listening to the bird's beautiful songs. They almost always sounded full of hope and love and happiness and meaning. They filled Adam with joy and a will to live.

Ben noticed that Adam looked happier when he sang. He wanted to see the boy happy, so he sang more and more. As the days passed, Adam felt the bird's song seep into his flesh and bones and give him strength and health. Adam's condition began to improve. Little by little, he grew stronger, healthier. One morning, he got out of bed, sat next to the window, and looked at the bird singing so joyfully outside.

When Adam's father came in to bring him breakfast, he was shocked. "Adam, what are you doing out of bed?" he cried. "You'll strain yourself!"

"No, Father, I'm feeling so much better!" Adam replied.

His father rushed over and kissed him, then ran downstairs and called the doctor. A few hours later, the doctor came to examine him again.

"It's a miracle!" he exclaimed. "Adam is getting better! I just can't understand it."

"I'll tell you how I got well," said Adam. He went to the window and pointed up at the singing bird. "Every day, when I listened to that bird, I felt better. That bird gave me back my health."

When Ben heard Adam's words, he was thrilled. He had helped cure a poor boy of a terrible disease!

Ben was so happy that he started singing as never before. He sang late into the night, until he wore himself out and slipped off into sleep.

The next morning, Adam's father said to his son, "Let's go out and feed that bird. That's how we'll thank him for saving your life."

They had no birdseed, so Adam crumbled up some bread and put it in a milk carton. He and his father walked out of the house and under the branches of the poplar tree.

"That's funny," remarked Adam's father. "I don't hear him singing now."

"He was singing all night," said Adam. "Maybe he's tired." Then he pointed. "Look, Father! The poor bird!"

There, on the ground, lay Ben. Adam's father bent over the small, crumpled form. "I'm afraid we can't thank him, Adam," he said. "He's gone."

"He's dead?" said Adam. "But he saved my life! He sang and sang for weeks and weeks, and he healed me. And now, this is his reward? Father, is that right? Is that fair?"

Adam's father put his arm around the weeping boy.

"Adam," he said softly, "we see only part of the story. We don't have the bigger picture. But we must believe that even when we don't understand it, everything God does is for the best."

At that moment, no longer imprisoned in the body of the bird, Ben's soul was flying straight to Heaven.

It was evening and it was morning,
the second day.

Day Three

THE THIRD MORNING was another sunny day as we continued with our new "routine."

Ellen and I had breakfast together, sitting on low chairs. We managed to finish eating before people began dropping in again. We discussed how we felt about the fact that our friends had moved the baby's crib out of the house.

It was out before we got back from the funeral. We both thought that was a smart idea, and we realized how lucky we were to have such a supportive community. Our friends were taking care of everything. All we had to take care of was ourselves and each other.

My father always told me that the most important

decision I would ever make was deciding whom to marry. That one choice would affect the rest of my life more than any other decision. I could see his point. It's one thing to choose someone to be with you for the good times, but when that person has to share the hard times, the heartrending times — that's for real, that's the true test.

The visits were good, the phone calls were supportive, but in the end we would be facing our tremendous loss alone and together. We would be left with the children we still had and a big, empty space in our lives. It was going to be a tough week, and so would the time after.

"How should we let your mom know about the baby?" I asked.

"I can't let it come from someone else," Ellen replied. "I have to be the one to tell her."

"Would it be best if we both go?"

"I think I should just go with my sister."

Ellen and her sister left the house that morning to visit her mother at the hospital. Traditionally the mourner doesn't leave the shiva house, but, in this case, tradition demanded it.

Ellen's mother was strong, and so were her daughters. But it wasn't easy. She cried. They cried. It hurt.

Ellen's mother died four months later, under a full moon, just as her granddaughter had.

"Are you afraid to die?" I asked Mr. Karasani, a very special person in my life.

I had always wanted to speak to him about the "D" word, as I had learned so much from him over the years, and this was as good a time as any. He had been overseas for the last few weeks and had just returned. Now he was here in my living room. Having someone like him spend time with me during the shiva was a tremendous boost.

He looked out the window and took a deep breath. "No, I'm not afraid to die. When the time comes, the time comes — and that time will come for every one of us. It's just a question of when."

He definitely had everyone's attention.

"It can be any time from the moment we are born, as we move closer, second by second, to what we call death. Dying is part of life. It's just that when it happens, it never seems to be the right time. We always think there will be a tomorrow. As a matter of fact, we like to think we'll live forever, and we refuse to think forever might actually come."

"Mr. Karasani, would it be fair to say that in my baby's case, 'forever' came a little too early?"

Everyone looked at me, utterly silent. I think we all agreed on the answer.

When things were quiet during the day and "traffic" was slow, my mind sometimes took me back in time.

Somehow, with all the confusion and bewilderment of what had happened, insights drawn from past encounters shone through. They helped.

A MOMENT OF LIFE

We hadn't slept in three days. As we came to the end of our winter maneuvers, the dust, dirt, and grime blended in with our bodies. There was no day or night. A bite to eat, pack up, regroup, and we were off again. I couldn't wait to finish, shower, and just sleep. The sounds of artillery shooting overhead didn't bother me. I could have slept through anything, given the chance.

Suddenly, a fighter jet swooped down on us, growing from a small speck in the sky to a mass of supersonic noise speeding right over our heads. I came to my senses immediately. But even then I was soon back on autopilot.

It was just past midnight on the last night. At 4:00 a.m. we would be done. There we were, in the middle of the desert, with all our war machines — thousands of tons of steel, their engines idling. It was a hot, dry, quiet night. Nearly everyone was sleeping. It was our last exercise.

Inside my carrier, it was hot and stuffy. The only light came from the radio dials glaring off our guns.

I couldn't breathe. I had to get some fresh air. I pushed the door and it flung open, then I stepped out into the crisp night. No one stirred inside. The 175-mm

Howitzer rumbled behind me, outlined in red cat's-eye lights. Behind it shimmered a seemingly endless array of mobile masses of steel, waiting for the word "Move!" A long line of little, red cat's eyes.

Let me just lie down for a minute, I thought. I looked up at the stars. There were zillions of them, each shining its pinprick of light into the universe. What a picture. Lying on the desert sand, I became part of the landscape. In less than a second, I was fast asleep.

My bed was about to become my grave. After the last machines had rolled over me, there would be nothing left. They would probably never find me. What a way to go.

I never heard the command to move, or the hundreds of thousands of horsepower surging forward.

Who is that pulling on my shoe? Opening my eyes, I discovered that the Howitzer that had been right behind me was now practically on top of me, very neatly nicking the tip of my boot. Such a delicate cut, just enough to wake me. Why the driver didn't go straight forward, I'll never know. Only the night noticed me as I leapt to my feet and started running after my carrier. The door was still hanging open as the vehicle lumbered on, and when I caught up with it, I jumped inside and closed the door. All my buddies were sound asleep. No one knew what had just happened. Within seconds I joined them in their symphony of slumber. Such a fine line had separated me from death — but apparently, it was not yet my time.

"Every one of us has a limited time in this world," Mr. Karasani continued. "We all know that. When a person dies at the ripe old age of, let's say, eighty-five, we say he lived a full life. He accomplished, became, did, achieved. When a person dies at thirty, we say he was snatched in the prime of his life, prematurely. We think about what he could have accomplished if only he had lived longer. When a child of seven dies...life can be so cruel, he was so young. When a baby dies at two months, what can you say?"

I took over. "Highway robbery. Senseless. Pointless. Why?"

"What you're really asking," observed Mr. Karasani, "is why are we so shaken at the death of an infant and so much more accepting of the death of an eighty-five-year-old. I think what really bothers us is that the gift of life was so fleeting. We think we know how long we should live. Why isn't life the way we expect it to be?

"If someone offered you a fully paid, two-week vacation, would you take it? How about one week? Three days? Even one day? Of course! 'No strings attached? Where do I sign?'

"If someone promised you a beautiful friendship that would last eighty-five years, would you take it? How about thirty years? Seven years? Three months, maybe even less? Of course, why not?

"We are given many gifts in this world. Should we be upset that some are short-term, or should we appreciate every day of that vacation or that friendship? What should we tell our kids? Maybe we should tell them to be thankful for every day, every hour, every minute."

"I hear what you're saying, but it is just so hard when the gift is taken away. It is just so hard. The mind doesn't rule the emotions. They rule," I confessed.

I thought to myself, *some special moments are worth a lifetime*. We've all experienced them: sitting mesmerized by the sea's endless waves; watching the sun set in a rainbow of purples and reds; savoring your child's smiles; being with the person you love more than anyone in the world; becoming a father, a mother, or better yet, a grandparent. Then you realize life is really great. Life is made up of these moments.

Mr. Karasani helped me realize that a lifetime of these highlights can be much shorter than other lifetimes — maybe just a few years, or months, or even less. This isn't easy to accept. Although it makes sense and I understand, I fight it.

And what about a person who experiences hardship, pain, illness, and torment? What about my baby, who never had a chance? As my friend Dean wrote in a beautiful note, "Such a sudden end to such innocence and love."

WHY?

The look in his eyes is one of betrayal. Fear...a blank stare of fear. How could you do this to me? I've known you my whole life! I always trusted you. I knew I could come to you whenever I needed anything. You were always there. You gave me all the love anyone could want …endless. Just tell me, how can you do this to me now? Why do you just sit there and say nothing?

The grip tightens.

The young boy closes his eyes and awaits the inevitable. He can't move. He has no one to turn to, not even the one to whom he owes his life, since that very person is holding him down.

If the boy only knew how much pain his father is in. His father knows that no explanation in the world would make any sense at this moment. How can he convey to his son that this vaccination is for his own good?

When it's over, they walk out of the clinic holding hands — one hand filled with unconditional love, the other with confusion. The father knows the chocolate marshmallow sundae waiting around the corner will soften the blow and set things back on course.

We want to be in control, to know all the answers — and right now. Why did she die? How could it have happened? It's scary not to know, because the consequences may not be in our favor, and it might even happen again. We get so involved with the why — and so much more with the how — that we forget we must now deal with the new reality. Will it change my life? How about my next few minutes?

I didn't have time for that, as I found our six-year-old sitting next to me. Emuna was more attached to the baby than any of our other children. She held her, changed her, put her to sleep...she was in love with her. Whatever the baby needed, if Emuna could provide it, she would. "How old was the baby?" she asked.

I was never good with ages. They just didn't register.

"You know what?" I suggested. "Bring over the calendar, and we'll figure it out."

In a second she was back. "From where do we start counting?"

"From here." I pointed to the box of Tuesday the fifth. "Do you want to count weeks or days?"

"There are more days than weeks, right?"

"Right."

"So let's count days. One, two, three, four, five, six, seven..."

When she got to thirty-one, she stopped.

"That's already more than a month."

She continued counting. Ellen was speaking with some friends across the room, but everyone focused on Emuna. The higher she counted, the more excited she became.

"Fifty-nine, sixty, sixty-one, sixty-two. That's more than two months! Sixty-three, sixty-four..."

Every day seemed so special. Emuna was counting up our baby's life. Where would she end up?

"Seventy-three, seventy-four..."

I put my finger on Sunday the nineteenth.

"Seventy-five, seventy-six."

Our fingers met.

"Wow, seventy-six days! That's a long time. She was seventy-six days old.

"Mommy, do you know how old the baby was? I know," she proclaimed, getting up to go over to Ellen.

How much does every day count? I thought. I did some quick calculations. What an impact a seventy-six-day-old baby was having on an almost 15,000-day-old father.

It was midday. There were just a few people in our living room when he came. Nathan is very shy, an introvert if ever I've known one, but he pulled up a chair and sat down right in front of me. I sensed this wasn't easy for him.

Nathan is tall, so when he bent over, his face was just a few inches from mine. He looked into my eyes and spoke softly, so only I could hear:

"I'm not sure you know, but I also lost a child many years ago. I can allow myself to say that I know how much it hurts, because I've been there.

"But listen to me. We were all given a very special gift that we have to be thankful for: We are able to forget. If we remembered everything, we wouldn't be able to live."

His eyes teared. "I'm telling you, don't worry, you'll

remember your daughter. But you'll also be able to for-get."

He sat there with his eyes closed for a few seconds. Then he reached over, squeezed my hand, and left. It hurt him so to come, but he had a priceless message to deliver. I was getting a lot of them lately.

Later that night, as quite a few people gathered around me, I received an overseas phone call. I had been on the phone around five minutes when he walked in.

Franklin. I wondered how he'd found out about the baby. We went back a long time. Franklin wasn't his real name, but when he'd shown up in class over two decades ago wearing those round Benjamin Franklin glasses, that was it. From then on, that was his name.

We'd shared lots of good times. We had chosen dif-ferent paths, but whenever we met over the years, we'd pick up where we left off. Franklin was into the "spiri-tual" life, traveling, disappearing for months. No one really knew what he did, and he always avoided the is-sue. I remembered hearing that he hardly slept any-more. I really wanted to speak to him.

As Franklin sat down in the back, our eyes met. The room kept filling up while I was still on the phone. When I finally finished the call, the conversation was mainly with the people sitting close to me. After ten minutes I noticed Franklin rise and walk toward the door. I couldn't get up and run after him. I quickly motioned to my brother to catch him and ask him to come back later. I didn't tell my brother to ask for Franklin's phone number. He wouldn't have left it anyway. That's just the way he is.

My brother came back after a few minutes and told me Franklin was very busy, but he would try his best to come, probably on the late side.

It was evening and it was morning,
the third day.

Day Four

THREE DAYS at home. I wanted to go outside, back to work. But was I ready? Far from it. I hadn't even scratched the surface. I was just getting used to the questions. I knew that if I walked out now, I would be carrying a lot of baggage with me, and I might never unpack it. Three days was not enough. Whom would I be fooling? For the time being, I knew my place was inside.

As the week wore on, people came and went, but time seemed to stand still. I felt I was bordering on another world. So much was happening: the talking, the listening, the questions, the searching for answers... but somehow time was different. I couldn't put my finger on it.

WORLD OF ANGELS III

*There are three partners in the creation of a person: the
father, the mother, and God. The parents contribute the
physical makeup — the bones and sinews, the flesh and
internal organs, the eyes, the hair, the fingernails. God
provides the soul, the spirit of life, the uniqueness and
beauty of the face, the ability to see, hear, smell, speak,
and walk, and the capabilities of understanding and
common sense.*

*When a person leaves this world, God takes back all
He gave, leaving the parents' contribution lying before
them. And they cry.*

*"Why do you cry?" God asks them. "I took only what
was Mine. I didn't touch what was yours."*

Mr. Karasani came again to see me on his way to
teach. I asked if he could help me piece together this
new sense of time.

He settled into his chair. "Do you remember a few
months ago when I spoke about the three most important days of your life? Do you remember what they
were?"

To my surprise, I did: "The day you're born, the day
you get married, and the day you meet the teacher who
can help you make the changes that will really make
the difference in your life."

"Did you ever think about why the day you die is
not on the list?" he asked. "It's a good question, no?

"I think you probably can understand better than

most people what I am about to say. Now listen carefully. The day you die, you enter a realm where time is different. Time doesn't exist there in an absolute sense. You have to realize that our time, the time we are experiencing right now, is just another creation, like the air or the mountains. When you die, you leave all that behind. You enter a dimension that cannot be defined in our terms."

"I'm with you so far."

"You get a taste of it when someone close to you dies. Since you were attached to his real being, his essence, the things that made his life worth living will remain with you. They'll cling to you like glitter. You understand that the person is no longer with you, but in fact he is still there. You'll be in touch with the real him and the real you. When that happens, you'll be brushing up against the next world, where days are not days, and everything's different.

"The day you die may be important to family and friends, but for you it's not really a day. It's simply the entry — or, more precisely, the *return* — to a world of truth, where there is no day or night, and where souls rule. It's the real world; the one we know deep inside is the destination of our life's journey, no matter how long or short that journey may be.

"I think one is especially conscious of this world when he's sitting shiva."

Bingo, I thought to myself as I recalled that first night and sitting alone in a dark room, with a candle being the only source of light.

Our tradition tells us that the first week after a person dies, his soul is confused. It wanders back and forth between the grave and the house where it so recently lived, not sure where to go — and leaving little sparks behind for the glitter-conscious.

I recalled Mr. Francis telling us at the funeral that in Jerusalem, where we live, it's customary for parents who've lost a baby not to attend the burial. Looking back, I could see the wisdom in it.

I think the reason babies are so cute is that they have nothing else to offer. Their existence may give you meaning, purpose, and joy, but it is all passive on their part.

When they learn to recognize you and give you that big, toothless smile, that's your reward for all the diapers and sleepless nights. When they try to communicate, you are in paradise. It becomes a two-way street.

All meaningful relationships are built on give-and-take. Otherwise, they don't last. Sometimes, one party seems to be doing all the giving, but if you look a little deeper, you'll see that, actually, in a truly meaningful relationship there are always two givers. Both sides give, and both take.

My baby was everything to me, but I was at a disadvantage. Apart from the opportunity to be a father, to grow, and to give, what had she given me? Of course, she was precious, by far the cutest thing on the planet, and she'd given me beautiful, priceless moments. But she wasn't able to reciprocate.

There are things she would have done in due time — like turning over in her crib and looking at me with those big eyes when I walked into her room, or saying, "Da-da," or running into the house after school and giving me a big hug. I never had any of that. The relationship was there on a certain level, but I was waiting, investing, and now I would never reap the fruits of my labor. Did I need closure? Yes...but by going to the burial, I would have been giving again, and it would have been too painful. That blue van which took her to the cemetery was taking her down a road that would lead me in the wrong direction. Giving for giving's sake is praiseworthy, but also going to the cemetery a few times a year would have left my cry unanswered. Of course, it hurt, but her soul did what it had to, and mine has to do what's right for the living. Everyone's has to.

It may sound cruel, but relationships that go nowhere are best left alone. Instead of walking around in pain for the rest of my life, I'll focus on my present existence, minus the gifts I've lost. I'll try to handle all the challenges with which I've been blessed. The pieces will fall into place one day.

Her leaving pains us. But really, we share the same reality: we are all souls. You realize that when you lose a baby. You look at the world differently.

Tears...tears mean change. After a good cry, you

sleep better. You let go of the confusion and make room for repair and growth. Pleasure comes through pain. Good morning, life.

Later in the afternoon, I found myself sitting across from Mr. Leifer, one of the most grounded people I know. He's always smiling. From speaking with him I could tell that it's so clear to him that people die. It isn't just theory. Just as you have ten fingers, you eat, walk, laugh, and cry...you also die. It's part of life.

Mr. Leifer left me with these thoughts: "The hard part is when death hits close to home. It hurts, and questions come flying at you from all sides. After the first few days of saying, 'It can't be. How can it be?' you turn to 'It was, and it is what I perceive it to be.' It then develops into 'How can I deal with it, since it did happen?' and then, 'I will start to live and grow from it.' It's not easy."

I could understand what he was saying. I just wasn't sure what shape I would be in when I would reach the acceptance stage. It wasn't going to be easy.

Mr. Leifer looked me in the eye. "My friend, if you can get up off the floor after seven days and say God loves you, has given you so much, cares for you and always has, then you've sat shiva. God gave you a precious gift, He entrusted you with her, and you watched over her. He chose you to enable her soul to achieve its purpose.

"You've had a special encounter that not everyone has. You must be special in God's eyes. I want you to know that good can come out of a house of mourning. You don't know how many people you can strengthen at this time. You're falling into what appears to be a big, black hole, but when you land, you won't be the person you were a week ago. You'll never be the same. If you really sit shiva, you can start to deal with the reality of life in the face of death."

I can still hear his words.

NEXT IN LINE, PLEASE

It was tall and majestic — the king of the forest. For as many years as I could remember, it had towered above the other trees as if it were their spokesman. The king seemed to protect them as they constantly strove to attain its height and breadth.

What a beautiful tree! It seemed destined to cast a shadow for eternity, giving so much. It protected the soil, sheltered animals, birds, and insects, provided shade and beautiful mats of leaves in the autumn, purified the air...a complete ecosystem.

Till one day it was felled.

All that beauty destroyed. Nothing would ever be the same.

But now the sun was able to reach places that had never seen the light of day. There were new spokesmen. It wasn't over. Some said the forest was safer now that the "king" was gone. Let the soil rejuvenate, they said.

The king was hauled in chains and trucked away, never to be seen again. The other trees never did find out what happened to it.

Normally, after a full life in which you've accumulated merits and demerits, you still need the family and friends you've left behind when you move on to the next world. They can improve your "placement" in that world. Acts of giving, helping, and caring, performed with the intent of benefitting the soul of the deceased, can help it find a better niche. We, the living, can make an impact. The connection is still there.

But my baby — she went right to the front of the class. She needs no assistance. She can't get any higher. There is nothing to mend, nothing to elevate. She left no unfinished business. It makes me feel good, but I still want to do something for her. After all, I am her father.

What can I do for my baby now? Would it really be a waste of time to try and help her? Maybe I can build or initiate something in her memory, so she won't be forgotten? Lots of lofty ideas go through my mind. But there's nothing I can do for her. That's the obtuse reality.

So how about moving on with my life and being the best person I can be? Not because she needs me to be, but because that's clearly the wisest and most effective thing to do. It just makes sense.

We all want to be needed, especially by our children. But now the roles have reversed. My infant daughter has become the wise adult, and I'm the helpless child. What would she want me to do now? What would we want for our other children? To grow up and make good decisions in life, to make those hard choices, the ones we avoid. To stand on their own two feet, look at the world around them, and start walking.

Slowly I found myself realizing how precious life is, and how time is constantly slipping away.

It was evening and it was morning,
the fourth day.

Day Five

MORE THAN halfway there. By the fifth day, I knew one thing for sure: After this was over, I wasn't going back to the old "normal." No, there was going to be a new normal from now on.

I was very touched that elderly Mr. and Mrs. Saffron, whom I've known for many years, came from quite a distance to see me. They could have called, as so many did. But they came.

"You know," Mrs. Saffron realized, "we never got to see the baby, as Murray hasn't been feeling well the last few months. Do you have a picture of her?"

I thought for a few seconds and then it hit me. "Actually, we don't have any good pictures of her. As a matter of fact, we hardly have any shots of her at all, and they all came out fuzzy. Really, every single one of them. We usually have enough pictures of the children in their first few months to make a full-length movie, but with her, we just don't. Isn't that strange?"

"That really is," she agreed.

"We don't even have an official birth certificate for her. We got them for all the other children right away. With her, don't ask me why, but we never got around to it. It's like she just slipped through the cracks."

Mr. Saffron leaned both hands on his cane. "It seems you won't have much to remember her by," he remarked sadly.

I thought of our baby. "No, I think she is definitely leaving her mark."

As I said these words, I could see Nathan sitting right in front of me two nights ago, saying, "Don't worry, you'll remember your daughter. But you'll also be able to forget."

I was starting to understand what he meant.

WORLD OF ANGELS IV

In a remote corner of southern Poland, in a marshy valley where the Sola River flows into the Vistula, about thirty miles west of Cracow, Heinrich Himmler decided to build a new prison camp for the Reich in the spring of 1940. The countryside surrounding the Carpathian foot-

hills was strangely beautiful, a mosaic of meadows speckled with wildflowers. His staff deemed the site forbidding, however. The water source was polluted, mosquitoes were everywhere, and the few existing structures were useless.

But Major Rudolph Hess saw things differently. The location had two important advantages. Though isolated, it had good railroad connections, and it was not open to outsiders' observation. "It was far away, in the back of beyond, in Poland," Hess recalled in his memoirs shortly before he was hanged in 1947. The Poles called the place Oswiecim; the Germans called it Auschwitz.

Auschwitz became a death camp, a facility whose sole purpose was to annihilate human beings, to turn something into nothing. It was governed by the principles of absolute evil; its function was death.

Max lived through Auschwitz. He rode the death train to the camp, survived the selection, saw the white-gloved hand of Dr. Josef Mengele wave him on to some sort of life, witnessed the gassings, the burnings, the killings, the deaths, the survival, and the liberation.

Max was a survivor but a destroyed man. He wouldn't talk about Auschwitz or about what he carried deep inside every moment, but it showed. The unspeakable was written all over him. He rarely smiled or exhibited any other emotion. Nor was he big on conversation; he kept pretty much to himself. People knew not to pry, to leave the past to his memory alone.

At the funeral of his three-year-old great-nephew, Sammy, who had been hit by a bus, Max sat up front, off to the side. Very few people noticed the tears in his eyes. Great-Uncle Max hadn't cried since the war, fifty years earlier. He had thought he had no tears left. But for his great-nephew he had tears. Something shifted inside him. Wheels stuck for half a century slowly began turning.

Max told his family that those few days Sammy had stayed with him during the last vacation had been his happiest time since the war. Sammy had brought him so much joy.

Only a little angel could have given so much pleasure to a man who had been through the unthinkable. A human being could not have accomplished that. Only an angel.

Was I the only one in the real world? All week, ever so gently, I seemed to be verging on a different place. I kept sensing I was on the outside looking in, but I couldn't touch the inside. It was a very strong feeling. I realized I'd had a brush with a new "time," but it wasn't just that.

As the father comes up to the window, he scans the newborns. They all look the same, but he finally sees the one with his chin. That's how they said he'd recognize him. No doubt about it, this one was his. The proud father gives a big smile, a little wave, and even mouths a few words to the baby, but through the window nothing is heard, seen, or felt. There's no physical connection. The baby is oblivious to it all, totally unaware even of his father, who helped create him.

It always strikes me when I see people wearing those shirts that look like they're inside out (sometimes they really are), with all the stitches and seams exposed. It looks a little rough, but I always notice that everything is being held together by those stitches. Without them, there is no shirt. The stitches and seams are the key to it all.

What really holds us together? What makes us who we are?

Imagine that behind or inside every person — the person sitting next to you, the person walking or driving by — a fine-lined shadow shows his stitches and seams. It follows his every movement. It's there all the time. It is his soul.

When he sleeps, it leaves him, but during every waking moment it's right there. You can't see it or touch it, but you know it's there. It manifests itself only through him — the real, complete person. To be oblivious to that "shadow," the essence of the person, is a crime. If we knew how to open our eyes, we would see it.

WORLD OF ANGELS V

The angel comes up to the chamber of souls and calls out to one soul in particular — which, like the rest, has been waiting since the beginning of time, when it was created — "It's your turn. You have to go down."

"Why must I leave this place?" the soul cries. "There's peace here, and truth, and all that is good. I want to stay!" It begs and pleads, but the angel dutifully sends the soul down into a body. Its stay may be long or short, and some come down more than once, but each one can't wait to return home. All souls have been around for thousands of years, and they'll continue to exist for a long, long time to come. We all get to meet some of them down here on earth.

WORLD OF ANGELS VI

I can't believe my parents decided to live in an earthquake zone! All these tremors are making me edgy. The world is so big; I can think of a million places to live rather than here. Just wait till I can make my own decisions. Go figure parents. The tremors are even waking me at night. I'm really trying my best to forget about them, but it's getting pretty difficult. My parents don't seem so worried about them. My mother gets a little more apprehensive than my father, but maybe that's just the way mothers are.

I think it would be easier to deal with my fears if I left the house more, but my parents feel home-schooling is best. The funny thing is, they're not the ones doing the teaching. They must have hired this teacher, and apparently they pay him very well. He's with me all day. I mean all day. I think he actually lives with us, or at least very close by. He must.

The first time we met, I asked, "What are you going to teach me?"

"I am going to prepare you for the big world out there," he answered. "I am going to give you the building blocks you'll need." I specifically remember those words. "If you listen to me and remember my words, you'll develop a strong foundation."

We've never looked back.

I don't know where my parents found this guy, but he really knows how to teach. He's clear, he makes sense, and I understand everything he says.

I also like him. He's always smiling, and there's this shine about him. We get along very well. I don't know how he holds my attention for so long, but he does.

I still remember our first meeting. He just sort of showed up. He felt right at home and made me feel very comfortable. He had this sparkle, that's really the best way to describe it. We clicked from the beginning. He was lucky, because I could have caused him trouble. My parents were always close by, but they never interfered. I guess they relied on him.

It's been over half a year that we've been learning together. I think maybe even a few months more. I've *lost track of time. The only thing that shakes me up and reminds me of the outside world are those tremors. They're actually getting stronger and much longer. But they never seem to worry my teacher.*

We touch on so much. The mechanics of the world, the makeup of people, relationships, the sciences, economics...everything. We cover a lot of ground.

He always stresses, "It's not such a big deal to learn. The real test is to remember what you've learned, so when the time comes, you can apply what you know."

I always answer, "I'll just call you up."

"And who says you'll find me when you need me?"

As more days, weeks, and months pass, I get a funny feeling we're not going to be learning together much longer.

"Till when did my parents hire you?" I ask one day.

"It's really not up to them," he replies, "but don't worry, it will be quite obvious when these sessions are over."

One lesson in particular really made an impression on me. He held his hands open: "As you go through life, remember to give. Be a giver." And then he closed them, making two fists: "Don't be a taker.

"The power and pleasure are in the giving," he explained, opening his hands again. "When you give, you'll be changing your life as well as the lives of others, and

you'll be rewarded many times over in return. But lest it go to your head, remember that you can always do much more than what people think or say you can. Then you'll accomplish even more and put everything that we've learned to better use. Do we have a deal? You'll be a giver?"

"It sounds easy. It even makes sense." But why did he want me to promise?

Wow! That tremor was at least a 6.0 on the Richter scale. The whole house shook! Things fell off the walls. This was no joke. My teacher had found the perfect time to make a deal.

Another one!

Everything started caving in. The tremors were now coming in waves, forcing me to the door, which happened to be the safest place to be. Maybe I could ride it out there. But till I got there!

I heard my mother screaming as never before. Someone yelled, "Push!" I guess he was trying to get out as well.

The teacher was still with me. Where he got his composure, I'll never know. "Remember what I've taught you, remember what you've learned. Building blocks...a foundation....All these months I've given you clarity. Hold on to it. Do we have a deal? Remember, look for your inner self and you'll find it all...."

"Okay, okay. But what good will it do me? I think it's all over!" I cried as I slipped away. "Help me!"

I flipped over onto my side and slid down the hall. Everything was moving with me. The whole house. We were goners.

At the last minute, the teacher stretched his hand out to me. He was going to save me! But he didn't. Instead, he just touched my upper lip, right under my nose.

Mission accomplished, the teacher looked on as the baby left the womb...out the door and into the world. The mother stopped screaming, and the baby picked up where she left off. And, lo and behold, both his hands were clenched in fists. The teacher smiled and nodded. With one touch, leaving an indentation in the middle of his upper lip, right under his nose, his student had forgotten everything he'd learned over the last nine months.

Now the baby had the rest of his life to remember what the angel, his teacher, had taught him. His soul had all the information. He just had to tap into it.

Every soul comes down to this world for a fraction of its immeasurable existence. Every soul knows that its return to the world of truth, and its place and form there, depends on its success in this world. Here the soul can be the motivating force, but it is not always so easy. The body it occupies can follow its own path. But when body and soul work together, united in purpose, both feel true bliss.

Sometimes, souls come down just to "tie up a few loose ends" left over from their last visit.

The soul knows that when it comes down to this world, it is starting its journey home. If only we could glimpse that world of souls, if only we could see every person's "shadow," things would be so different.

Sometimes we do have that privilege.

Close your eyes and imagine yourself with family and friends. Think of all the reasons you love them, all their good points. Now visualize that shadow behind each one of them, that source of goodness following them around. That's why you love them. The world is filled with souls. When a magician reaches into a hat, turns it inside out, and says, "See, nothing inside!" you know he's lying. Something is there; you just can't see it.

We need to refocus. To ignore this reality would be a big mistake. If we could just hold on to our image of people's souls, we would see everyone in a new light. We would see the whole world differently.

I saw my infant daughter differently as the days went by. Sitting on the floor, I came to know her better, and she helped me to better understand myself.

Among the paperwork we received from the hospital was a printout of some 26,000 little squares forming a grid. At one end it said, "3:00 p.m.," and running right down the middle was a blue line. The line quivered slightly but was basically straight. It sort of died out in the middle, but about 3,000 squares later it came back. It stopped abruptly where the paper had been ripped.

My baby's heart wasn't giving off a reading. It couldn't make that line move. That fine line separated her life from our world. I would have given anything to jolt that line into a sharp zigzag.

I heard about a young girl who, after heart surgery, found herself hovering above the operating table, watching her own body being worked on. She briefly left this world but came back to describe how she'd felt and what she'd seen. "I suddenly realized I could see myself on the operating table below," she said later. "They couldn't get my heart to beat. It seemed strange to see my own body down there, but it wasn't frightening...."

My baby took her experience with her. I think I know what she saw, but I want to know what she felt.

How does it happen? How do souls depart from the body? How do they leave this world? Through the halt of blood circulation? Inadequate oxygenation? The flickering out of brain function? Organ failure? The destruction of vital centers? These are the weapons wielded by the angel of death; his methods of delivery are unlimited.

That's the way we usually look at mortality — as the body's inability to overcome disease or other catastrophe. But there's another way to view the departure from this world: The soul is simply recalled to the world of souls, because its mission is over. This exit can be difficult and painful, like a knotted rope being yanked through an undersized hole, cutting and chafing as it passes through to the other side. Or the transition can be smooth and peaceful, leaving no traces. This is the "kiss" of death.

When the shadow quietly moves on, it's a sign that the soul was leading. Gently and silently it became partners with the body, and gently and silently it departed. We think the angel of death comes to kill, but, in fact, it comes to reclaim the soul. It all depends on how you look at life and death. It's that simple — and that crucial.

On that first night, when I sat alone in my living room but felt I wasn't alone, I believe it was my own shadow I was feeling, as well as my daughter's. Call it shadow consciousness, or glitter consciousness. I was sensing that the essence of a person is elusive and certainly not what we see. I am now starting to understand that there really is meaning in loss.

As the day drew to a close, someone mentioned the date. Both Ellen and I realized at the same time: what a way to spend our anniversary.

It was evening and it was morning,
the fifth day.

Day Six

I WAS EMOTIONALLY and physically drained, and it was not getting any easier. With just two days left, more and more people were visiting. Those who came now were certainly seeing a different person than those who'd visited a few days before. The hard questions kept knocking. They wouldn't go away. Why her? Why now? Why us? What now? The terrain was becoming familiar.

Shifra came home all excited. Our four-year-old was having such a good time in kindergarten and at her friend's house during the week. She was too young to understand.

"They're coming! They're coming!" she cried, running over to Ellen.

"Who's coming?"

"My teacher, and Emuna's teacher and Tehilla's teacher. Everyone's teacher!"

Sure enough, all three teachers soon filed in. They spent about fifteen minutes with Ellen, speaking about the baby and the children.

When they left, Ellen said, "They're not just teachers. They all came as mothers."

Whenever I looked over at my wife that week, I thought I couldn't possibly be feeling the same pain she was. She'd given birth to the baby. She'd carried her for nine months and cared for her afterward.

I once suffered such severe back pain that I was beside myself. I can take pain, but this was a quantum leap from anything I had ever experienced. The doctor came to the house and I overheard him telling my wife that the spasms that I was experiencing were pretty close to the pain of childbirth. But only "pretty close." Ellen had experienced more. How could I ever have the same relationship she had with the baby after what she had gone through?

Her loss was my loss, and her baby was my baby... but it couldn't be the same. The cry of a mother is not the cry of a father. It can't be.

Each of us talked with friends and visitors throughout the day. Sometimes there were more than forty people in our living room, not to mention all the phone calls. We really didn't have much time for each other, and by the end of each day we were asleep before our heads hit our pillows.

I never expected to meet the doctor who'd answered the call in the ambulance. But Dr. Dana introduced himself and sat down in front of me.

"I hope you don't mind my asking," I began, "but if you can remember, what was going through your mind on the way to our house? You knew it was a baby, right?"

"That was one of the first things we were told, and whenever we know that, it's hard. We all tried to prepare ourselves emotionally on the way, because when we arrive at the scene, we have to detach ourselves from the fact that we are treating a baby. It's always very difficult to see an infant in distress. We all have children...."

"And when you saw her, did you think you had a chance?"

"I always feel there is a chance. We did all we could to get a pulse and get her to breathe, but we couldn't. I thought the hospital might be able to succeed, so we rushed her there."

"Did you really think she could pull through?" I pressed. "After all that time without a pulse?"

"If I had thought it was hopeless, I would have stopped everything right there at the house. I wouldn't have continued trying to save her. It wouldn't have been right to continue with all the procedures. It would have hurt her."

"What do you mean? If she was no longer alive, how could you have hurt her?"

Dr. Dana looked uncomfortable. "You and I don't know what she was feeling after she died," he said quietly. "What exactly happens after death, I'm not sure. I'm only a doctor.

"But I know there was more to her than just her little body, and I wasn't going to hurt her unless I thought we had a chance to get her to breathe. That would have been wrong. Somehow she would have felt pain. But don't ask exactly how or what."

I swallowed hard. "Dr. Dana, where do you think she is now?"

"Mr. Clyman, I truly believe your baby is in a place that's good. Totally good."

Dr. Dana received a message on his beeper and rose to leave. One last question:

"Doctor, have you ever saved babies who were in the same situation mine was?"

He paused to think. "Yes, I have. And again, I'm sorry that with your baby we couldn't. I guess sometimes we have to realize that it is not in our hands."

The beeper beeped again, and I could see that his mind was already somewhere else as he hurried off.

There is a tradition that one should leave a cemetery by a different route than he entered. I was given a beautiful insight into this custom. When you go to a cemetery and stand at a gravesite, so close to death, it has to make an impact. You should come away changed. That's the symbolism of exiting a different way.

Something had lingered in the back of my mind for the past few days. I tried not to think about it. I was afraid to, as I knew this was self-incriminating territory, but it wouldn't go away. I didn't discuss it with anyone, but I kept wondering. Had the baby passed away because of something I had done? There would certainly be no better way to punish me. Just take away the most precious thing I have. Make it really hurt.

A father has every right to cry over the loss of his baby, but after many years and much thinking, I look at the passing of my child as a window of opportunity. It forced me to introspect. If my actions or thoughts had even the slightest connection with what caused me to lose her, that loss brought me closer to myself. I had no one else to look to.

I fell into a turbulent sea of thoughts and tears that spanned the gulf between where I was and where I should be — and where I could be. Deep down, you know where you could be. In this vast sea of self-awareness, you either sink or swim. You can also float or tread water, moving in no particular direction, but not for long.

The bottom line is that you want to move, you want to change. The water can be cold, and you can stay frozen without moving from your present location for years — or it can be so hot that you'll do anything to get out, but you may not end up heading in the right direction. But you want to live! Don't let the water temperature fool you. Do whatever you have to do to change. Don't get caught up in your surroundings. It's a choice between sinking and swimming.

When you realize the huge gap between yourself and your goal, you wake up. Enough apathy and defensiveness — let's see some positive action. The sea of change is big, deep, and uninviting. You feel out of your element there. You hope and grope for complacency, for some island where you can just sit on the beach with a favorite drink and a good book and relax. But no, from out of nowhere – WHAM! Sometimes you can't get much farther away from that tranquil vision. But that's when you surface and start swimming to the other side.

Maybe if I hadn't been thrown overboard into the ocean of tears, I would never have known I was on the wrong side. Now that I know, I'm crying and I'm changing. I'm free.

Did I have to have such a rude awakening? I'm still thinking about that. And my baby; she came and went, and I outlived her, but she outdid me. To do such a thing to a parent requires a unique connection. I will do my best not to let her down.

I'm going to swim. One stroke after another. When I get into a rhythm, I'll begin to cut the water, leaving behind barely a ripple and a few bubbles. I can do it. It's just a matter of deciding to live.

I take a deep breath, lift an arm over my head, pull into the water, and start kicking....I'm starting to move. It's hard, but I know I'm getting that much closer to the other side. I sense the beginning of a breakthrough.

My baby is cheering for me. I can't hear her, but the noise is deafening as she leads thousands of angels.

It was evening and it was morning,
the sixth day.

Day Seven

"SETH, I THINK someone's at the door. I don't believe it. Who could it be at this hour?"

"What time is it?" I could hardly open my eyes.

"Three forty-five in the morning," Ellen answered.

"Unbelievable....Maybe someone's in trouble. Let me go see who it is." I shuffled through the living room in the dark.

"Who's there?"

"It's me, Franklin."

"Franklin!" I exclaimed as I opened the door. "Are you early for tomorrow or late from yesterday?"

"I told your brother to tell you that if I could make it, I would be late," he said earnestly. "He told you, didn't he?"

"Yes, he did. But still…"

"And anyway, I saw the light on."

What light? All I saw was the memorial candle we had lit almost a week ago.

I guess he was right. The light was on.

For the first few minutes, we updated each other on what had happened in our lives since we'd last met over two years ago. Then:

"Franklin, give me your angle on what life is putting us through in this house. I know you see things a bit differently than I would. You always have."

"It's not my angle, it's just what is. A person can see what he wants to see. But that doesn't mean there isn't more to it than that."

"You mean like souls?" I asked.

"I see you've been doing some thinking. That's just part of it."

"Listen, the sun's coming up in a little less than three hours. Get yourself a hot drink, and let's start talking." He came back with two cups of tea.

We spoke till dawn. It was quality time, and a lot of my thoughts over the past few days got slightly polished. They were still far from gems, but they were becoming a little less rough around the edges.

In our nocturnal journey, we touched on the baby's dying under a full moon — an auspicious time, a time of goodness and inspiration. With this energy we started the week of shiva.

We spoke about sitting low all week, if not on the ground, identifying with where my baby was and what that was doing to me. We noted how sitting low is humbling. If you want to change, humility is a good place to start.

We spoke about the seven days of Creation and the seven days of shiva.

We saw how seven symbolizes unification, the big picture. Only with a sense of that, can we begin integrating what we feel and observe, and then, hopefully, we can eventually give back. Our seven days would be the first unit of time that would give us the power and tools to better understand what life had recently dealt us, and how to continue.

We touched on the World to Come and realized it exists now, not in the future; we are just not part of it yet.

We were fascinated by the power and beauty of the soul and the possibility of harnessing it.

The hours we spent together helped put me in touch with what I had been feeling. I wish I had taped our conversation, as it was really too much to fully absorb.

To my surprise, Franklin asked many questions as well: How I was coping? What were my thoughts and conflicts? How strong was my faith? How were Ellen and the children faring?

Franklin hadn't changed. Deep down, he remained

the same sensitive, caring person, but he certainly marched to his own drummer. I thinked we clicked because we were so different. He was a good friend. I knew that if I needed anything, I could count on him. The only trouble would be finding him. Just one thing left me puzzled. It was truly puzzling that he still wasn't married. I know he wanted to be and had come very close a few times. He would make such a great husband and father. He was made for the part.

Before we knew it, the dawn was sneaking up behind the mountains outside. I could still get in an hour of sleep if I was lucky, or else it would be a rough last day.

As Franklin got up to leave, he looked at me. "Seth, I have to be truthful with you. When I came the first time, at the beginning of the week, it was for you. But tonight I came here for myself."

"What do you mean?"

"When I heard you and Ellen had lost your baby, I was devastated. When I came to your house a few days ago, I was glad you didn't have time for me. I heard you on the phone and talking with people. That was enough for me. I knew you would be able to weather this. You didn't need to speak to me. I would just add color. But when your brother told me you wanted to see me, I figured it was really a sign that I needed to see you."

As I said, Franklin always saw things differently than I did.

"So before I came tonight, I tried to think about

what you could give me. What did I need to hear from you?

"You told me how you and your family were struggling to keep sane when your world seemed so cruel and meaningless. It would be so easy just to think about yourselves, move to a new place, and start over. But instead, you sit here in your home with people day in, day out. You talk to them, exposing your confusion, facing it again and again. That's brave. You didn't blink."

"Thanks, Franklin, but I don't follow."

"Don't you see how much good is coming out of this house? Just think how differently parents are going to look at their children and at each other after coming here. Your lives will certainly change, but so will many others. You are giving them gold, pure gold. Don't you see? Your baby's death is triggering so many emotions, pushing so many buttons, releasing so much energy. All these things together could literally blow you apart. And who knows how long it would take to put the pieces back together? But look, you're turning this whole 'tragedy' around.

"You're making sure your baby is leaving behind a better world. She didn't die for nothing. Her death shouldn't just be depressing. What a waste if that were all that came out of it. Instead, it should generate something positive, something good."

"You are definitely putting everything in a different light."

"Seth, I want you to know — and you know I avoid the topic, but believe me when I say it: I'm associated with some very powerful people. They may be motivated by money and power, which may not always be coming from the right place, but they can move mountains if they want to. They have the means. But trust me, you have more power than they do. You are truly blessed. You're so lucky."

I felt a big lump in my throat.

"Everyone has his challenges, and everyone thinks his is the ultimate. But being here with you helps put things in perspective. Still, it's so hard to change. It's easy to teach, easy to preach, but it's so hard to change. Even just a little."

As his eyes went misty I realized he was truly talking to the both of us.

"I envy you so much. To be married, with a family. What I wouldn't give just to have my own child, even briefly. Just like yours."

As the sun broke over the mountains and the room slowly lit up, we hugged. It just happened.

"Thanks for opening the door when I knocked," Franklin said. "You know, I think that deep down I was hoping no one would answer."

"You can thank my wife for that. She's the one who heard you. I was out like a light."

"I'm also sorry for coming so late. It was just hard

for me. I was sitting in my car down the street for a long time until I could bring myself to show up here."

As he was leaving, he turned around. "Could you do me a favor?"

"Sure."

"When you have God's ear, could you put in a good word for me? And tell Him I'm trying."

Just as I went back to sleep, Ellen woke up.

"Who was that at the door?" she asked.

"It was Franklin."

"Why did he come so late? Couldn't he have chosen a better time?"

I don't think she realized that that was a few hours ago.

I thought for a second as my eyes closed. "No, I think he came right on time."

The morning of the last day. The week was coming to an end. Seven days. Soon I would be leaving the confines of my house, my private world for the past week, to reenter the bigger one outside.

After hearing me talk with some visitors, a good friend who had come by quite often during the week commented, "I don't know if you realize it, but you've changed a lot in just a few days. I feel it. Compared to the beginning of the week, I see more confidence in you. You seem more grounded.

"The things you're saying are very powerful, and I don't know if you've noticed, but people are listening. I'm not sure who's comforting whom."

I thought of Franklin.

Still, whenever there was a lull in the action, it would hit me again. While I had been at work, miles away from home, the angel of death had come down to earth. Of all the billions of people in the world, the angel came to my baby daughter and told her soul it was time to move on: "Your job is done here. Just leave the body where it is. They'll find 'her' in an hour, when it's time for her feeding. Don't worry about the parents. They'll figure it out. They'll be hurt, but they won't let you down. Just keep focused on the big picture. Let's go."

My friend Ian told me that when he lost his father, he and his mother had sat shiva. Many thoughts were shared throughout the week, but his mother just sat on the side in her own world, saying very little. On the fourth day, an older gentleman came to visit and noticed she wasn't part of the conversation. He picked up on the distress of a woman who'd been married more than fifty years. "Don't worry," he told her. "You'll see him again."

For the first time that week, she smiled. That's what she'd needed to hear.

As the last day wound down, I kept asking myself: Why am I still alive? What is my purpose? How do I fit into the big picture?

I've come to realize that the real tragedy is not what we suffer, but what we miss out on. There are things we don't even try to do but we could have, times we should have known better but chose not to, people we could have been but weren't. That is worth crying over.

WORLD OF ANGELS VII

At age ten, Paul ran into the kitchen and slipped on the wet floor. He landed on his stomach so hard that he ruptured his spleen. He swelled with fluids and went into shock from internal bleeding. His parents rushed him to the hospital, where his heart stopped. This is what he experienced:

"I left my body, although I still felt connected to it by a string. I floated up to a corner of the room and watched as three doctors worked frantically to rescue me. I was sure I was going to die, and I have to admit I found their efforts to save me kind of funny.

"I then went down a long tunnel and approached a warm light. At the other end of the tunnel, a being greeted me.

"The greeter was not physical, but more a feeling, or an awareness. He told me I couldn't stay in the tunnel. I could either go back or continue, never to return.

"I didn't actually decide to go back, but I sensed from the greeter that there was a purpose to my life.

"While I was thinking about whether to stay or return, I felt myself enter my body.

"For a while I longed for that light. Then I realized that someday I would see it again. In the meantime, I had things to do."

By the end of the week, through my exhaustion, I was anticipating my "landing." I wanted to go outside and walk in the sun.

Reentry

IT WAS THE strangest thing. The week before my daughter passed away — or should I say, moved on — my car got two flat tires. It was a little disturbing, but what can you do? My luck.

So when my good friend Yale came on the last day and told me, "You know, your back left wheel is flat," I couldn't believe it.

Yale came that day because it's customary that someone actually tell you to get up from shiva. A week is enough.

"You know, Seth, this has been quite a week for you," he commented. "You look like you've been pretty roughed up."

"Yale, only a good friend could say that. But I want you to know that I really tried to handle the week and not let it bowl me over. You won't believe what helped me.

"When I was a teenager, I played a lot of sports with my neighbor across the street, Steve. He was a real jock, great at any sport, and I was his punching bag. He was older, stronger, quicker — you name it, he had it on me. He literally wiped the floor with me. But my luck, he really liked me. I guess he sort of looked at me as a younger brother. He didn't have one.

"When I would catch his baseball pitches, you could hear the smack of the ball in my glove all over the neighborhood, and did it hurt! When I caught the footballs he threw, they knocked the wind out of me, and when he would tackle me, forget it. When we played basketball, I took plenty of hard elbows and had my share of chipped teeth. This went on for years. I kept at it and, in the end, before I moved away, I started to beat him. The school of hard knocks had forced me to meet the challenge. Steve was even more surprised than I was, and I think that deep down he even enjoyed it.

"You're right, this week has really wiped me out. If you think I look roughed up now, you should have seen me a few days ago. But you know what? I'm going to win. It took me years to beat Steve, but I finally did. And I'll beat this, too. And this time," I added, thinking of my baby, "it's not just a game."

"Seth, I don't think it's supposed to happen this

way, but you're making me feel better..."

I felt there was something that he wanted to tell me, but he couldn't get it out.

"Yale, is something bothering you?"

"Yeah," he replied uneasily. "You remember when you called me from the hospital right after your baby died?"

"Yes."

"Well, I wasn't sure what to say. But when I told you, 'I guess God didn't want her to live anymore,' I think I was out of line. The words just sort of came out. I should have realized that it might have been easy for me to say but devastating for you to hear. I'm sorry for being insensitive." He looked down. "I really can't believe I said that."

"Yale, we go back a long time. Don't worry. You didn't say anything wrong, and I wasn't hurt. I mean it."

"All I know is that if it had been me, I don't know how I would have taken it."

After a few seconds of silence, he looked up at me.

"You know what?" I said with a smile. "Even if I had trouble hearing it then, I've had a whole week to sit on it."

"I guess you have," Yale replied, nodding.

It was time. I was ready.

Yale stood up, stepped back, and said, "Get up."

I reached out for his hand.

No sooner had I gotten up from shiva than I was outside changing a tire. What's the message here? Who knows? But one thing I realized then and there was that if I was serious about moving on with life, I had to get down to work and, if need be, get my hands dirty. It can be hard and, at times, confusing. It may hurt, and I might even get roughed up, but I have to move on.

We all need to move forward and face our challenges; otherwise, we're moving backward. We don't want that for our children, and we don't want that for ourselves.

Driving to the garage on the spare to fix the flat, everything seemed the same yet different. I couldn't put my finger on the difference.

As I drove, I thought of an old parable: Behind every blade of grass stands an angel telling it to grow. Every blade. Everyone and everything has a "sponsor."

I was suddenly very aware of this truth, but I wasn't sure the driver in front of me was. That was it: I was glitter-conscious! Soul-conscious! I remembered that first night of shiva, alone in the living room with the candle.

I had completed a weeklong crash course on awareness: of the shadows beyond our view, the deep seas we must cross, the tears of change, and the Creator of bodies and souls who cares for every one of us. I needed to remember and assimilate these life lessons in order to continue my quest. I'd never had a better chance.

Waiting
for
Whispers

A SUCCESSFUL YOUNG executive was driving down a neighborhood street, going a bit too fast in his new Jaguar. He watched for kids darting out from between parked cars and slowed down whenever he thought he saw someone.

As he sped along, no children appeared. Instead, a brick smashed into the Jag's door! After slamming on the brakes, he then backed up the car to the spot from which the brick had been thrown. He jumped out of the car and grabbed the kid standing there, pushing him against the parked car.

"What do you think you're doing, boy?" he demanded. A head of steam building up, he continued rav-

ing, "This is a new car, and that brick you threw is going to cost me a lot of money! Why'd you do it?"

"Please, sir, please, I'm sorry. I didn't know what else to do," pleaded the youngster. "I threw the brick because no one else would stop...." Tears streamed down the boy's face as he pointed to the other side of the parked car. "It's my brother, sir," he continued. "He rolled off the curb and fell out of his wheelchair, and I can't lift him. Would you please help me sit him back up? He's hurt, and he's too heavy for me."

Moved beyond words, the driver tried to swallow the rapidly swelling lump in his throat. He lifted the boy's brother into the wheelchair, then took out his handkerchief and cleaned him up.

"Thank you, sir, and God bless you!" gushed the grateful child.

As the young executive watched, the little boy pushed his brother home. It was a long, slow walk back to his Jaguar.

He never did repair the door. He left the dent there to remind himself not to go through life so fast that someone has to throw a brick at him to get his attention.

God whispers in our souls and speaks to our hearts. Sometimes, when we don't take the time to listen, He might just throw a brick at us.

It's our choice. Listen to the whisper...or wait for the brick.

Years
Later...

WE'VE NEVER BEEN to our daughter's grave. My children have never even asked to see it. Where is she buried? Somewhere in Jerusalem. I might even have walked right by that little bundle of mine. She never flashed me that toothless smile, never called me Daddy, never gave me a big hug. I never got to take her hand as my father always did with me, saying, "Let's walk down the path of life together, just you and me." But she sure taught her old man well. She opened me up to a whole new world.

We'll all get to that World to Come, the world of answers instead of questions, the world of glittering souls. We'll all meet again. That's a promise. I'll reunite with my baby. She'll greet me with that smile I so long to see. And when that time comes, I'll probably be surprised to see how much she's grown.

A Note for the Bereaved

THE HARDEST PART of dealing with my daughter's death was bridging the gap between her intangible world and our here and now. In this book, I've tried to describe the challenge and provide some tools to help bring these two worlds closer. Take the time to think about them, and be real with your thoughts — as real as you are with your loss. That loss was precious; your thoughts are even more so.

You can be a victim of fate or the architect of a new destiny. It's up to you.

Getting up off the floor is never easy. To come out stronger, no matter how long it takes after such a devastating blow is even harder. It takes courage. I wish you that, along with hope, strength, consolation, and reward in your growth.

Sincerely,

Rena's father

Credits

DAY 2

Page 54: "A Children's Story," based on "Menashe and the Bird," in Sheryl Prenzlau, *Everything under the Sun*, Targum Press, 1993.

DAY 5

Page 86: "In a remote corner..." — Otto Friedrich, *The Kingdom of Auschwitz*, HarperPerennial, 1994.

Page 96: "I suddenly realized..." — Melvin Morse, *Closer to the Light*, Ivy Books, 1990.

Page 96: "Through the halt..." — Sherwin B. Nuland, *How We Die*, Knopf, 1994.

DAY 7

Page 115: "At age ten..." — Melvin Morse, *Closer to the Light*, Ivy Books, 1990.